What's Your Coffee Strategy by Rasool Muttalib Published by Bad Geek
Publishing 2870 Peachtree Rd #827 Atlanta, GA 30305

www.thecoffeestrategybook.com

www.badgeekmedia.com

First Edition

ISBN-13: 978-0692730133 (Bad Geek Publishing)

ISBN-10: 0692730133

Table of Contents

Chapter 1

The Coffeehouse - The New Center of the Universe

There have always been power centers in society - places where people commonly go to wheel and deal. It shifts from place to place based on the times, evolving cultural DNA, and the underlying technology driving both.

Ultimately power centers are defined as the places people go to make important decisions. The more decisions made in a particular place, the more of a power center it becomes. With the emergence of mobile technology - laptops, smart phones, free-Wi-Fi – and the confluence of shifting social norms - the need to be hyper-productive (caffeine), the new individuality, and the need for quick 'any-time' social spaces to meet with others to discuss business, life, or meet new clients - the coffeehouse is now fixed squarely at the epicenter of the modern decision making world. *The coffeehouse is the new center of the universe* - not just in the United States, but all over the world.

How Decisions Are Made - The Power of Relationships

I read a story about Mike Muhney, the co-inventor of ACT!, the Contact Management Software. He learned his first relationship-lesson very early in his career when he was an IBM salesman in northern Indiana. One day he contacted a CEO, presumably for a big sale, who told him "Mike, I'd like to talk with you, but I'm literally getting ready to go on a two-week skiing vacation. Feel free to contact me when I get back." When Muhney followed up three weeks later, quite naturally he asked how the vacation went. What he didn't know, and to his surprise, not a single one of his competitors did the same. The CEO said "Your competitors have all contacted me since I've been back from my vacation, and none except you asked how it went. What that tells me is you're a professional, you care about me, and I do not like to talk with amateurs. Let's set up a meeting." You can guess what happened next. All of the competitors were shot down, and Muhney ended up making the sale. He said later about the deal, "IBM taught us, what's on the walls? See the trophies, the pictures, the evidence of the things they love. When you get them talking about the things they love, it builds trust." And that, is how some of the biggest decisions are made.

The fundamental key to accomplishing your goals is to influence the decisions surrounding those goals. The challenge is, as seen in Muhney's story, decisions are not always made based on objective thinking. In fact, the underlying drivers behind most key decisions, both in business and life, are based more on

When dealing with people, remember you are not dealing with creatures of logic, but creatures of emotion."

— Dale Carnegie

the relationships between the people involved than any factual information that might be available. Who gets promoted, who wins the contract, which strategy gets adopted, which proposal gets approved, all of these important and potentially life-changing decisions are based more on relationships than anything else. Understanding this reality makes establishing and cultivating relationships with the right people not only the most important part of influencing decisions, but also the single most important part of accomplishing any goal you set out to achieve.

How the Coffee Conversation Builds Strong Relationships

One of the first questions most people often ask is, "Why is the Coffee Conversation so different?" and "Why is it so effective when compared to any other conversation?"

The Coffee Conversation is the modern way to connect with new people, build relationships,

Coffee conversations are brief, in-and-out, low-risk/low-commitment sessions which makes them the most effective method for building relationships, your personal brand, and gaining support for key decisions

and is altogether different from any of the more formal dinner or lunch engagement methods we have become accustomed to. It's more open, more personal, and even amongst co-workers there is a tendency to let their guard down which gives way to a more personal conversation. These exchanges allow you to establish relationships that are much deeper than if the same discussion would have taken place at the job, in an office, or in some other formal venue. The personal connections you establish in these brief, seemingly insignificant conversations are very powerful and can last well beyond the current job, contract, or decision-point you are meeting to discuss. This is the hallmark of creating influence, driving key decisions, and accomplishing the goals you set out to achieve. For the purpose of gaining support, meeting new people, and strengthening relationships, the coffeehouse has no equal.

Why a Coffee Meetup Instead of a Dinner Invitation?

Over the past 20 years, the attention span of the average adult has gotten smaller and smaller. We consume information at a much more rapid pace and in smaller chunks than ever before. We only want the essential facts to make a decision - lose the extra fluff. This is what makes the coffee conversation so powerful. Coffee Conversations are brief, in-and-out, low-risk/low-commitment sessions which makes them the most effective modern method for building relationships, your personal brand, and gaining support for key decisions. Most people will accept an invitation for a coffee meeting because it fits perfectly with todays' fast-pace, quick soundbite culture. A person having to leave after a 10-minute chat is just as normal as a person leaving after an

"Be amusing: never tell unkind stories; above all, never tell long ones."

— Benjamin Disraeli

hour. It all depends on how the conversation flows. There is no long-winded commitment like with dinner invitations. If there is no energy – either person can casually 'go to their next engagement' without feeling trapped or offending the other.

The Coffeehouse as Your Personal Headquarters

While sitting in a coffeehouse writing this book, I overheard a conversation between two strangers. One person walks by, and the classic circumstance of two people who haven't seen each other in years running into one another unfolds. They spent the standard 5-10 minutes catching up on what's been going on in each others' lives – personal, career, travel, etc... After the reunion ended, the person sitting next to me overheard the conversation and happened to be looking for someone in that exact line of work. She introduced herself, they had a brief conversation, set an appointment, exchanged contact information, and just like that – someone has a new client for their business! If you aren't using the coffeehouse as your personal headquarters, you just aren't doing it right.

The Coffeehouse Gives Time & Space

In order to plan, engage, and strategize effectively you will need time and space – physically and mentally. When you come into the coffeehouse, you have both in abundance. You can disappear amongst the chatter of the people and clanking coffee mugs into your own personal world. You can fully immerse yourself into your thoughts and ideas without distraction.

When the time comes, you can then invite the important people you want to meet to familiar territory. Feeling comfortable and knowing the landscape can give you a personal advantage in any engagement. It also helps with building credibility if you know the baristas by name and they also know you. It shows you are respected and acknowledged by others. Which in turn, makes others inclined to give you that same level of respect without knowing very much about you.

The coffeehouse is the perfect meetup for so many different types of objectives.

- **At Work**: It provides a stronger sense of personalization. As discussed, you will find in the atmosphere the coffeehouse creates, coworkers are more inclined to loosen-up and be more candid outside of the office. It also creates a stronger sense of bonding amongst the people involved. For key relationships you want to build, invite coworkers to get a cup of coffee at the local coffeehouse.
- **With a Client**: You will find it so much easier to invite potential clients and other people you want to meet to a local

coffeehouse. The environment is considered 'neutral', and the other person knows they can leave at any time without offending. Your invite-acceptance rate will increase many times over when the invitation is just 'over a cup of coffee'.

Not to mention there is always the possibility of stumbling upon new business or key contacts by having friendly chats within earshot of others.

By Yourself: You can be completely alone and uninterrupted in the coffeehouse. Everyone somehow knows when you are in the mode of wanting to be within your own space. Almost as if a virtual 'Do Not Disturb' sign is up at exactly the right time so you can be completely engaged in whatever you are doing.

KEY LESSONS

- Power centers are places where people go to make important decisions.

- The coffeehouse has become the new center of the universe where important decisions are made every day.

- People will accept a coffee invite more willingly than any of the more traditional invitation types.

- Some of the most important decisions are made based purely on the relationships of the people involved, even when others are more qualified or better options are available.

- The coffeehouse is the perfect place to establish and develop relationships with co-workers, clients, and anyone else you would like to meet.

- Make the coffeehouse your personal 'headquarters'. You will be amazed at the quality of work you can complete and opportunities that present themselves just from intermingling with others.

Chapter 2

What is the Coffee Strategy?

In anything you do or work to achieve, the best methods for accomplishing what you are after are normally exactly that.....methods. A repeatable formula or framework that can be used over and over to accomplish the same results. That is exactly what the Coffee Strategy is. A well-defined, efficient, repeatable methodology that uses the coffeehouse as a central headquarters for accomplishing any goal in your life – career, business, or personal. It is a powerful strategy you can use again and again to achieve success in all of your endeavors. The best part is, the more you use it, the better you will become at repeating success.

The sheer number of things we all have in our sights to accomplish in life are far too

Coffee Strategy: The Coffee Strategy is a well-defined, efficiently structured, repeatable model that uses the coffeehouse as a central headquarters for accomplishing any goal in your life – career, business, or personal.

"We are what we repeatedly do, excellence then is not an act, but a habit."
— Aristotle

many to enumerate. From losing weight, to purchasing a home, to starting a business, to spending more time with family, to going back to school, to..., and to...., and to...., the list goes on and on. Any attempt to create a unique method for each and every goal we have in life would be preposterous and completely unachievable.

The Coffee Strategy is a very simple, yet powerful methodology and is made up of three major phases. The idea is to use each one of them in sequence which will allow you to identify your goals, and then build a powerful strategy around how you intend to accomplish them. It was designed to be universal and can be used for almost any goal you can imagine.

The Coffee Strategy

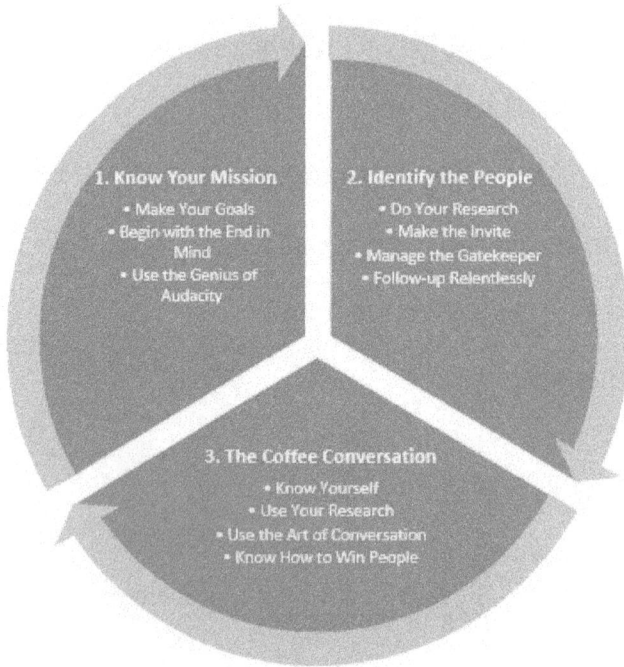

1. Know Your Mission
- Make Your Goals
- Begin with the End in Mind
- Use the Genius of Audacity

2. Identify the People
- Do Your Research
- Make the Invite
- Manage the Gatekeeper
- Follow-up Relentlessly

3. The Coffee Conversation
- Know Yourself
- Use Your Research
- Use the Art of Conversation
- Know How to Win People

Below is a brief outline of the three phases of the Coffee Strategy. You will read more detail about each phase in the subsequent chapters.

Know Your Mission

This is all about identifying the goal. What it is you are after. It could be anything. The key is to understand that in order to accomplish anything you have to identify exactly what success looks like. You will understand the meaning of 'exactly' once you read Chapter 3. Once you complete this step, it makes mapping out a clear path and the process of getting there much easier.

Identify Who Can Help You Get There

The second step is one that so many people overlook. There is a tendency in all of us to believe that we can 'go it alone'. Accomplish all of our dreams completely on our own steam. In some cases, there is even a feeling that asking for help, or reaching out to others is a sign of weakness. This couldn't be further from the truth.

"Alone we can do so little; together we can do so much."

— *Helen Keller*

The real story is, the most successful people in life are the ones who understand how to establish and cultivate the right relationships to help them achieve their goals. Almost nothing of value is ever accomplished in complete isolation. At some point we will all need others to aid in pushing our ideas along, to make the right connections, and to help us accomplish the numerous things we strive to achieve in our lives.

Having the foresight to identify exactly who those people are and putting a strategy around the right time and place to meet them is more than half of what is required to get you where you want to go.

Connect with the People You Need

This is where you will actually use the coffee conversation as a critical piece in the process. Everything was paperwork and checklists up to this point. You have identified your goals and who will be needed to make those a reality, the last step is setting up the meetings and actually making connections with the right people to persuade them, gain their

You can have brilliant ideas, but if you can't get them across, your ideas won't get you anywhere.

— Lee Iacocca

buy-in, and come to an agreement that your mission is worth their support.

The challenge is, how many of us like sitting down with strangers for the purpose of persuading them to do something they may not necessarily want to do? Chapter 5 not only walks through the strategic aspects of why this is necessary, but also explains step-by-step how to develop and use the communication skills needed to be successful.

The most powerful advantage of the Coffee Strategy is you can take any goal you are striving to achieve, plug it in, and come out with almost surefire success every time. Once you complete this process a few times, you will see your confidence increasing exponentially which will make each progressive step along the journey even easier to achieve.

KEY LESSONS

- The Coffee Strategy is a modern methodology for using the coffeehouse as a central headquarters for accomplishing any goal you set out to achieve.

- The more you use it, the better you will become at accomplishing your goals.

- The Coffee Strategy has three major parts:

  - Know Your Mission

  - Identify Who You Need

  - Connect with the People

- The more you use the Coffee Strategy, the more confidence you will gain in achieving your goals.

Chapter 3

Know Your Mission

The most fundamental piece of your entire Coffee Strategy is knowing what you are trying to achieve. You have to define 'true north' to know which way is up. In other words, you have to know where you want to go. But there is one additional key to this seemingly basic part of your planning, almost a secret, and one that most people miss. Your goal must be very, **very** specific. In fact, your goal must be so specific you can visualize in your mind exactly what it looks like, feels like, even - in certain cases - smells like. If it's a job, you know exactly what job, the exact title, who will be working for you, where your office will be, what you will do every day.

Your destination, your goal, must be very, very specific. In fact, your goal must be so specific, you can visualize in your mind exactly what it looks like, feels like, even (in certain cases) smells like.

"The indispensable first step to getting the things you want out of life is this: decide what you want."

— Ben Stein

This point absolutely CANNOT be understated. It has to be so clear in your mind that every detail is visually at your disposal. Think about it, before you set out on any journey, whether it be a simple errand or an actual road trip from one city to another, you will always need a very specific destination in mind - maybe it's your friends' house, or the hotel in the city where you are going on vacation. It has an exact address, you probably know what it looks like, what to expect when you get there, you've already thought through and visualized almost every detail without even thinking about it. This is the destination where, once reached, you will consider the objective of that specific mission accomplished - and then you start a new one.

This is the key to success in any endeavor you undertake. The interesting thing is, if you really think back hard enough, the times when you unintentionally did this in your life are probably the times when you accomplished exactly what you set out to achieve. You just didn't realize you used this method. You didn't 'package it up' and present it back to yourself as a formula, or a methodology you could continue to use throughout your life to achieve literally anything you set your mind to. But that's exactly what it is – and now you know how to repeat this process at any time to your advantage.

Before you begin this journey, understand that the emphasis you place on contemplating your goals and objectives should be in direct proportion to the goals' importance and overall impact on you and your future. Said differently, the more impactful the goal, the more time

"Most of what we say and do is not essential. If you can eliminate it, you'll have more time, and more tranquility. Ask yourself at every moment, 'Is this necessary?'"

— Marcus Aurelius, Meditations

you should spend planning and orchestrating how you will be successful.

Those of you who have gone through this process before may be familiar with the entire goal setting process, so you may want to jump straight to it. Keep in mind these are not "New Year's Resolutions". These are life goals, career goals, things you want to accomplish in your life that will either continue, accelerate, or altogether change the fundamental direction you are headed in and place you on a clear course to your desired destination. So now the fun part. Let's break down the entire process piece-by-piece and get started on your goal-setting journey.

Step 1: Identify Your Specific Goal

Begin with the End in Mind

The key is to remember that with goal creation, you have to begin with the end in mind. Before you start to lay out the smaller projects, meetings, tasks, you must first determine exactly what the end-game looks like - just like a road trip. The more specific the better. If it's career, you might say, "I want to be a Manager, Director, or Vice President." Then you would add-on to that ".....of such-and-such department", to make it specific, or of "such-and-such" type of business, with "such-and-such" responsibilities.

If it's a business, you might say "I want to launch an online clothing business selling women's purses." Then you would add-on to that "....and I want to concentrate in

"Dreaming is not enough. You have to go a step further and use your imagination to visualize, with intent! Forget everything you've ever been taught, and believe it will happen, just as you imagined it. That is the secret. That is the mystery of life."

— Christine Anderson

such-and-such fashion genre with sales of such-and-such amount in the first year, and such-and-such amount in 5 years."

So now you are beginning to get the point, and it makes perfect sense when you think about it. For example, you are not just launching an online clothing business. Anyone can do that. You want YOUR online clothing business to accomplish a certain objective and probably more specifically, in a certain fashion space and only when that specific thing happens will you feel like you have made it to your first destination. Otherwise you might accomplish the 'task' of launching the website and you may even begin celebrating that accomplishment......but with no vision of how to attract visitors, no expectation for sales, and no further plan of action. Yippee!

The destination has to be specific. And you must begin with the end in mind. There are a few questions that can help you get started to help you hone-in on exactly what it is you want to do. If you aren't entirely clear don't worry, you're not alone. In fact, you are in the majority. In so many cases, we have been limping along in our lives for so long that we forgot to take a moment to think about what it is that **we** actually want in life. This is not unusual. So embrace the fact that you are opening a new door, or better put, re-opening the door that will lead you to where YOU want to go. And always remember, everything is possible. The secret to achieving it lies in the planning and the unrelenting amount of effort you will put forward to achieve what you have planned.

"Decide upon your major definite purpose in life and then organize all your activities around it."

— Brian Tracy

Below are some questions to help get you started. You can use these or any others to help you figure out exactly what you want to achieve. If you already have something in mind, this process will be much easier. If you are starting from scratch, these questions are a good place to start. In either case, remember to be very very specific, do not limit yourself, and spend an appropriate amount of time to make think through what you are going to commit yourself to.

Questions to Guide your Goal-Setting Process

- What do you love?

- What are you passionate about, what would you do for free?

- What type of career/position do you really want?

- What do you really want to do?

- What is your desired outcome - More freedom? More money? More personal fulfillment?

- What are you trying to achieve?

- What does it look like when you win?

Step 2: Brainstorm: Write Everything Down

You will definitely want to go to the coffeehouse to do this. Get a chair somewhere on the side. Maybe put on some headphones to allow yourself to be isolated in your own thoughts. Whatever the case is you need to be in the right mental-mode and place where you will not be disturbed to complete a quality brainstorm session. Do not leave anything unstated. This entire session is about writing down what you want to accomplish. There are no limits. Write

"The best way to have a good idea is to have a lot of ideas."

— Dr. Linus Pauling

everything. Document all of your goals and objectives. This will help you visualize what you are trying to accomplish. You will begin to see patterns, similarities, and relationships between some of the things you write. This is good because it means you leaning in a common direction where many of these goals can be accomplished along the way.

There are numerous methods for brainstorming. You are free to use one method that works best for you. To help get you started, I will outline one of the methods I have used successfully many times that I find to be both easy to follow and effective when using the results. Remember, everyone's mind functions slightly differently depending on a wide variety of things – a person can be more of a creative-type (right brain) or a logical-type (left brain). And a million other variables from background, culture, likes, dislikes, etc. So for this step, I invite you to either use the format I outline below, or to go online to find one of the countless other methods that might be more effective for you. The goal here is to get as many of your goals on paper as possible. So long as you do that, you have accomplished what this step is designed to achieve.

5 Basic Steps to Successful Brainstorming

1. Clearly define the topic to be brainstormed.
   - Remember to be as specific as possible on your goal.
2. Understand the objectives of your ideas

- What are you solving or trying to accomplish?
- Make sure your thoughts and ideas center around these things.

3. Aim to generate as many ideas as possible in 20-30 minutes.
   - It's ok to go slightly over if the ideas are flowing.
   - The key is to give yourself a time limit which creates a mental sense of urgency.

4. Don't change, criticize or evaluate any idea.
   - Just write.
   - Don't stop to think about whether or not each idea is valid, good, bad, or in-between.

5. Evaluate Results
   - Now go back and begin to put thought into what you have written.
   - Separate the solid ideas from the 'blabber'.
   - You can also combine ideas where it makes sense.

> - The goal is to end this phase
>   with a solid set of ideas to
>   move forward with.

Step 3: Categorize Your Goals

This is important because some of the goals you write down will actually be a part, or a sub-part, of other goals you already have. For example, if your objective is to start an online clothing company you might also have written 'launch a website', or 'find a supplier', or 'order business cards'. But when you take a step back, you'll see that these goals are just smaller parts of the main goal which is to start an online clothing company. This is not the same as having one goal to start an online clothing company, and another goal to lose 35lbs. Those two are not necessarily connected, but both may be part of your long-term strategy to change your life and accomplish your broader objective. That is, maybe you feel like one of the key parts of you being considered for that next position or launching your own business is being in better shape and having a better personal image. In this case, these two goals are related and a part of you being able to achieve your broader goal, but are not necessarily related in and of themselves. Your categories might be 'Launch the Online Store' and 'Get in Shape', and each one of those would have sub-goals you have identified to accomplish them.

The other powerful thing about creating categories is it allows you to visualize

"To accomplish great things we must first dream, then visualize, then plan...believe....act!"

— Alfred A. Montapert

and think through the sub-goals and necessary steps you would have otherwise missed to achieve your larger purpose. You begin to drill-in and think in specific terms of how you are going to pull this off. No more free-wheeling fantasies and daydreams. This puts you at the grassroots-level of actually getting this done. And this is exactly where you want to be.

Step 4: Prioritize and Rank Your Goals

In order to do this effectively, you will need to use some basic criteria in order to determine which goals are more important than others.

- Which goals are the most important?
- Which goals are the most impactful?
- Which goals will take the most time to complete?

As with all of the other steps, you'll want to put some thought into this. Take your time. You have to begin to think in terms of "bang for your buck". Which one of these goals will get you the farthest down the path of where you want to go. Some of your goals might be what are called "nice to have's". These types of goals can be understood as something you would really like to do, but not necessarily mission-critical to achieving your actual desired outcome. An example might be you want to join a specific social club, sticking with our earlier example let's say it's 'The Local Society of Online Retailers'. You are joining this interest group to gain insight from others in the industry, build your network, and get some exposure. This is in fact an important goal but might not be as important as completing your business plan, or identifying how you will be funded, or calling that person that told you some time ago "…when you're ready to start your business, I'll back you.", or some other goal that needs to be achieved in order to get your business off the ground. The idea is you have to put things in relative order of impact, priority, and importance to your overall game plan. All of the goals you write down are technically in and of themselves "important". But in relative terms, some will be more important than others – and that is the distinction you have to make in order to complete this step successfully.

Step 5: Timeline & Sequence

Now that you know all of the goals you want to accomplish, you've categorized them into themes, and prioritized in order of importance. The final step is to map out the order in which you will complete your goals. Now you begin to see how all of this comes together. You also begin to realize how others who have achieved great success in their lives and careers have accomplished it. Nothing is by accident or just happens. Most of the major success of the people we envy has knowingly or unknowingly followed this model of thinking. And now you have it right in front of you.

In plotting out the sequence of your goals, some will naturally come before others. Some that are short-term and happen quickly, aren't always first on the list. The key to this step is to lay out a natural sequence of events that is realistic, allows you to build momentum (example - you might place a few of the easier goals in the front to get yourself going), and puts you in the mindset and overall pattern of living and completing tasks and knocking-down your goals.

Momentum is also something that cannot be overlooked. You'll be surprised that once you get into a pattern of marking goals completed, your level of focus and overall sense of purpose and determination will increase. Your confidence will grow, and you will begin to feel better about yourself, your journey, and the ultimate success of your mission.

In terms of timeline, there also may be cases where one goal needs to happen, or makes more sense to happen, before another one - even if the other goal takes less time to complete. Remember, this isn't a race. You are mapping out a strategy to accomplish something altogether new and important. This plan will propel you forward in the direction that you've always wanted to go and set you on a course for almost surefire success. Just like in a normal game of chess, it takes patience, planning, and a little good fortune, but it somehow all comes together in the end.

Step 4: Identify the People

Now that you know what you want to accomplish, here comes the second most important component of your overall strategy. I can almost guarantee you, this is where 99.99% of people completely go off track. This is, and has always been one of the most important factors in accomplishing anything you will ever want to achieve in life. Connecting with the right people. Look at each one of your goals and identify who you will need to help you get there.

"Relationships are all there is. Everything in the universe only exists because it is in relationship to everything else. Nothing exists in isolation. We

have to stop pretending we are individuals that can

go it alone."   *- Margaret Wheatley*

Don't fool yourself. No one accomplishes anything alone. And relationships, building them and cultivating them, is the single most powerful thing you will ever do to help yourself accomplish anything in life.

As you look at your goals and begin to think about names of people that can help you, there are a few key things you'll want to keep in mind

> 1. You don't have to actually know, or be in *current* contact with all of the people you will need to help you. You just need to write down who they are.
>
> 2. There can be multiple people that you identify to help you accomplish each one of the goals you outline. It can even be general.

For example, if the goal is to lose weight the person you might identify is a 'personal trainer' – no name attached.

3. Don't shy away from putting anyone down on the list. But keep a couple of points in mind. If you need a one-on-one meeting with the President of the United States to accomplish your goal, well....that probably isn't going to happen. So you have to keep some boundaries of reality in place when you are putting your list together. At the same time, don't limit yourself or shy away from people that are realistically within your reach but might require a little effort to get a meeting with. You'll be surprised how willing and happy some 'important people' are to give

advice, offer help, and assist in the journey of an up-and-comer on the rise (we'll discuss more on how to do that in Chapter 4).

You're Done.

Wow! What an exercise. If you didn't complete everything and you actually want to achieve these major goals in your life, here is a reality check. Don't kid yourself. A great mentor once told me "Everyone loves to play. Champions love to practice."

Suffice it to say, there are no shortcuts in greatness. There are definitely no shortcuts in accomplishing major goals in your life. Most battles are won and lost before they are ever fought. It all comes down to preparation and planning prior to the event. Maximum input yields maximum output. Never ever forget that. You will be surprised to know how many people at

"If the people knew how hard I had to work to gain my mastery, it wouldn't seem wonderful at all."

— Michelangelo

every layer of business and society do not live by this rule and continue to be out-executed, out-planned, and out-maneuvered by those that do. Everyone can win now and then. The great ones win most of the time. Not always because they are better, faster, or smarter – but because they take the time to plan and execute a well-orchestrated strategy. Net-net, take this step seriously and do not engage in your plan without following through with it 100%. This is literally where almost all people derail themselves and end up not getting the results they are looking for. Now that you have the formula, just imagine how far ahead of the crowd you will be - almost every time.

Go forth and conquer.

KEY LESSONS

- You must identify very clearly what your goal is before you begin. So clearly, you know exactly what it looks, smells, and feels like.

- The Outline:
    - Begin with the End in Mind
    - Brainstorm – Write Everything Down
    - Categorize Your Goals
    - Create a Sequence to Outline the Order of Achieving

- Understand the Importance of People

- Identify Who You Will Need to Win

Chapter 4

How to Win People

Why People Are Important

People are the single most important aspect of successfully executing your game plan. Obviously the most important thing is knowing where you want to go and mapping out how you plan on getting there. After that, three words – people, people, people.

As we mentioned earlier, the very nature of many of the pioneering ambitious, entrepreneurial, trail-blazing types is they want to do it alone. "Everyone else will just get in the way" they say. Or "Maybe they won't understand what I'm after and will just slow me down…" Or some other statement along these lines. As such, they toil away for countless hours and days trying

47

to accomplish every single task, make every single connection, and knock down every single door, completely and entirely by themselves.

Ever heard of the story of John Henry? This is a classic tale of trying to work hard as opposed to using all of the tools at your disposal to work smart. John Henry was a steel-driver for the Chesapeake & Ohio Railroad back before they had steam engine drills to chomp through the hard rocks and do the job people once had to do with hammers and pick-axes. But he refused to believe that the steam engine could do the same job he could, so he took up a challenge to beat the steam engine in a race. Who won? Doesn't really matter when you consider the outcome. John Henry killed himself trying to win. That story is an exact parallel to this situation. Understanding and using people to help you along your way is so critically fundamental to your success. You may not actually kill yourself, but you certainly might kill your ideas and your dreams trying to go it alone. Three simple words – don't do it.

So now the question becomes, how do you go about engaging the right people at the right time? Moreover, how do you get them to help you? I mean, this is a rough world we live in. Who would willingly spend their time helping someone else?

All good questions, but here is the amazing thing. There are so many people who have achieved some level of success that absolutely love helping others. These people are all over the place. They all have different motives. There are some that just like to be thought of as someone who *could* help someone else, and they do it out of personal

49

pride. There are a million reasons, none of which should really matter to you. The important thing is they are out there, and available, *and* waiting to be asked for help. Take advantage of it.

Why engage people? Think back to the introduction. The most common driver of decisions is relationships. If a person knows another person, they will be much more inclined to give that person a chance. Or give that persons' friend a chance. That 'chance' might be your big break, your company winning the contract, your proposal getting approved, or you getting promoted into that new job. In so many cases, the only thing most of us need is that *one* chance and we can take it from there. Engaging people to help build bridges and open doors is the smartest way to go about accomplishing getting that chance. No matter how much you want to do it alone, how good you are, or what your goals might be.

If you didn't already know the importance of relationships, I think you do now. The next chapter will walk through what you actually do when you get in the meeting with the person you are trying to connect with. For right now, there are a few critical points to understand when thinking about engaging people that will allow you to be successful. If you don't go into this area of your strategy understanding and adopting these points, there is a very high probability your engagement strategy will backfire, which, in some cases, can be worse than never having engaged at all.

Six Steps to Get a Meeting with Anyone

1. Always Think Win/Win

This is the first point mentioned and also the most important. Sometimes we fall under the impression that in business and in life you have to 'take' whatever you can from whoever you can to get where you are trying to go. Often times, someone with this understanding will achieve some level of success. But it will also in many cases, be very short-lived. Or, when they fall into a slump, which everyone does, the people they 'used' on their way up will be nowhere in sight or refuse to offer assistance. Even worse, when they fall on hard times, others will get some enjoyment from seeing them fail.

"Lots of people want to ride with you in the limo, but what you want is someone who will take the bus with you when the limo breaks down."

— Oprah Winfrey

You obviously do not want to fall into this category. When you take a hard look at the people that have sustained success over long periods of time, you will see a common theme. They have solid relationships with a large group of very diverse and well connected people. Doesn't mean they know each other's children and visit each other for the holidays. It means, they both uphold a high level of integrity in the relationship, don't abuse it, and seek ways to strengthen it when the opportunity arises.

How do you do this? It's very simple. You have to always be thinking "win/win".

"When he took time to help the man up the mountain, lo, he scaled it himself."

— Tibetan Proverb

Thinking win/win appeals to your better side. Whenever you are embarking on a mission and you follow the formula by identifying the people you will need, you should immediately begin to ask yourself, "What can *they* get out this?" Or "What are *their* interests, and how can I help *them*?" As we mentioned before, there are people out there who may help just out of a personal good-nature. But there are definitely people out there who will help, if they also feel like there is some level of mutual benefit. Here is a rule of thumb you want to live by — **Always bring something to the table**. In sales they have ABC (Always Be Closing). If you are unfamiliar with ABC, take a moment and look up "Glengarry Glen Ross Alec Baldwin Speech" on. In this methodology, there is an equally important maxim you must follow — **ABG — Always Be Giving**.

ABG puts you in a position of being in demand. You don't want to be the person that every time your name appears on the Caller-ID, the other person thinks "What do they need now?" If you take the ABG approach, that means you have benefited from the relationship, but you have also allowed others to benefit from you. It doesn't always mean you are able to offer up a connection or a resource, especially when

"I don't know what your destiny will be, but one thing I know: The ones among you who will be really happy are those who have sought and found how to serve."

— Albert Schweitzer

the other person is much more established than you. It could be something as simple as offering up your time to support something the other person is involved in. The best way to find this out is to ask. In the course of the conversation, and in many cases before you get to your 'ask', you'll want to find out the other persons' interests, goals, or objectives and then figure out how you plug-in.

Just as it is critically important for you to know the right mentality to have in encounters, it can be equally important to understand what mentality to avoid. Or at minimum, be aware of the alternatives so you can recognize when you are falling into the wrong mindset.

According to Stephen Covey and many other brilliant minds on the subject of interpersonal relationships, there are 5 forms of human interaction. I will include a brief summary of each just to provide the full perspective.

1. **Win-Lose:** This is the most common understanding in business and many relationships. It means, one party must win at the expense of the others. In sports this is natural, one team wins, and the other loses. But in relationships and endeavors (unless you are competing with another party for a contract, job, or client) there should always be an opportunity for mutual gain. Either short, or long-term.

2. **Lose-Win:** This should be avoided at all costs. This is the mentality of a person that says "You win, I will lose.", "Take advantage of me, I'm a martyr.", "It really doesn't matter, I just want to keep the peace." They put

in time and effort and seek nothing in return. Usually this is because they don't know what they are after and/or have no real objectives. You may not think you are this person, but maybe you are.

3. **Lose-Lose**: This interaction occurs when two people are at odds. They would rather see the other person or party lose, even if it means they lose at the same time. It can be considered the "If I can't have it, no one will" mentality. The mutually destructive nature is completely intentional in most cases.

4. **Win**: This interaction occurs when the person operating with this paradigm says "I want to win. I don't want you to lose, but getting what you want is your business, not mine."

They do not actively seek to ensure that the interests of the other party are considered.

5. **Win or Leave It Entirely**: This is actually not a 'bad' alternative and might actually be used from time to time. This form of interaction essentially says, if we both cannot come away from this with some form of mutual benefit, let's not do the deal and come back in the future when something better is available. Not a bad way to maintain a relationship and both parties will respect each other much more than they did prior.

Now we move to our second principle of winning people. Once you have identified the people you want to connect with, the question becomes 'How do you actually do it?'

2. Do Your Research

After you have identified the people that will give you the best chance of succeeding, you don't want to simply set up the meeting and sit-down to begin a 'general' conversation. This entire endeavor is far too important and critical to be left to chance. The next thing you'll want to do is conduct some research on the person prior to meeting them.

"If I always appear prepared, it is because before entering an undertaking, I have meditated long and have foreseen what might occur. It is not genius where reveals to me suddenly and secretly what I should do in circumstances unexpected by others; it is thought and preparation."   *- Napoleon Bonaparte*

Doing research on others used to be a very difficult endeavor. But today with all of the social media outlets, this is easier to do now than ever before. In days past you would have had to figure out friends and acquaintances to glean, or even bribe for information. Today, it might be as simple as logging on to LinkedIn, Facebook, Twitter, and other social outlets to get a general sense of the person's interests. On these platforms you will find a treasure-trove of information regarding career history, hobbies, clubs, family, vacations, books read, colleges attended, etc., etc. etc. With the information you find, you will begin to create a profile of the individual that will serve as your base of research.

After completing the personal outline, you will conduct some extended research on some of the things you found. For example, if they are involved in a charity, or serve on the board of a particular group, go to the website of that group to find their mission, what they do. Maybe there is something you can do to help. Can get help with a critical project? As you begin to put together your strategy, these are all valuable nuggets to have in your conversation with the individual.

The most important thing is; from this information you begin to understand more about the person. You begin to see ways you might be able to help them 'win'. And believe it or not, almost everyone likes someone who has taken the time to learn about their accomplishments and discusses them with the person by way of compliment – "…I saw that you were the President of Sales at YZ Corp and you broke the record for revenue in a region. How did you pull that off?" This old-school flattery, when done in good taste and not over-schmoozing which makes a person suspicious, actually helps to loosen up a person. It makes them laugh a little and causes their guard to let down. Remember, with the overwhelming majority of people –

"The best salespeople are great listeners—that's how you find out what the buyer wants."

— Larry Wilson and Spencer Johnson

a favor given is one to be returned – even a compliment. Do your research.

3. Take Action

The next two steps are critical points where the goals of so many aspiring to carry out their plans comes to a screeching halt. The major reason? I guess you could call it "cold feet'. You might find yourself sitting at the other end of the phone, all digits dialed-in, and all you have to do is press the green 'Call' button – and you freeze. Or maybe the perfect introductory email is written, you have reviewed it so many times, and all you have to do is click 'Send' – and you can't.

Needless to say, you absolutely <u>cannot</u> do this. Procrastination kills all. It has been the most destructive common denominator for keeping hidden so many of life's would-be treasures that never made it to see the light of day. Don't let it do the same to yours.

"Action may not always bring happiness, but there is no happiness without action."

— William James

"There is nothing more difficult to take in hand, more perilous to conduct, or more uncertain in its success, than to take the lead in the introduction of a new order of things."

— Niccolo Machiavelli The Prince (1532)

Now that you've made your plan, time to take action.

4. Make the Invite

First things first. You've identified all of the people you need to meet and now you are staring at the first person on the list. What do you do? It's quite simple – you make the invite. Trust your plan. Trust your preparation. And move ahead with confidence. That person certainly is not going to call you first!

"The dangers of life are infinite, and among them is safety."
— Goethe

Depending on the type of person you are trying to meet, you may have to go through a few layers in order to reach them, and that is perfectly ok. Be prepared for that (we talk about 'Managing the Gatekeepers' a few sections ahead). As many have quoted, the journey of one-thousand miles begins with a single step. Take a deep breath, buckle-up, press 'Call' or click 'Send', and prepare for the ride of your life. It all starts here – Make the Invite!

5. Follow-Up Relentlessly

Well you didn't expect it to be as easy as just reaching out and clicking "Send", did you? Almost nothing worth anything in life comes easy. It is entirely possible that the person you reach out to does not respond. Maybe they are currently buried with work. Maybe they didn't feel like meeting anyone new at the time. Or, maybe they were in a bad mood.

"Let me tell you the secret that has led to my goal. My strength lies solely in my tenacity."

Louis Pasteur

Whatever the reason, you sent the invite and didn't get a return call or an email response. They say you don't become a salesperson until you get the first 'No'. And that statement could not be truer, especially in this scenario. If this entire process were easy, everyone would do it! Step outside of your comfort zone and follow-up if you do not receive feedback. Let them know you are important and you are willing to fight for their time. In some ways they will respect that and gain a certain level of respect for you, even though they may not know you. Don't become a pest, but also don't be ashamed to follow-up. Remember, in some cases these people can be the very keys that unlock the doors to your dreams – to *your* life's goals and ambitions. Don't let a 'first-pass No' demotivate or otherwise discourage you from moving forward. Follow-up Relentlessly.

6. Manage the Gate Keeper

There is something to be known about people who have established themselves. There is usually a gatekeeper. A gatekeeper is the person the individual you are trying to contact uses as a trusted advisor, a proxy, or as a second-set of eyes for important decisions. And they will usually take that persons advice and value their opinions. The gatekeeper is responsible for many deals getting approved, and for many people getting their 'shot'. One mistake people make is not understanding the value, importance, and influence of the gatekeeper. This person might be a close friend, an administrative assistant, or a business partner. You'll want to figure out who this person is so when you come in contact with them you understand who you are dealing with. They are normally not as accomplished as the person you are hoping to meet, they might be an employee, and they may not be as educated or accomplished as you are. But they are powerful…..very, very powerful.

The good news is they are normally not very difficult to get along with. They value and respect very highly those who show value and respect towards them. Do the same level of research on them as you have done on your primary target. Establish a relationship with them over time. Give them compliments and engage them in conversation. Ask for their opinion on things. Don't go too far, but you get the point. The person you are trying to meet will ask them what they think of you. Or, the gatekeeper might just offer-up their opinion. In either case, you'll want to be on the good side of that conversation. Many others will not. Most people see gatekeepers as an inconvenience and treat them in a dismissive condescending fashion. Never ever do this. You will be miles ahead of the game.

KEY LESSONS

- People are the single most important aspect of successfully executing your game plan.

- Never build alone.

- Take advantage of the numerous people out there waiting to be asked for help.

- Always think Win/Win when engaging someone else as a part of your strategy.

- ABG (Always Be Giving) - Always have something you are bringing to the table - no matter how small.

- ABG puts you in the position of being 'in-demand' where people will look to return your calls or include you in opportunities.

- The 6 Must Do's to Win Anyone

  1. Think Win/Win

  2. Do Your Research

  3. Take Action

  4. Make the Invite

  5. Follow-up Relentlessly

  6. Manage the Gatekeeper

Chapter 5

The Coffee Conversation – Connect with People Instantly.

The Blueprint of a Winning Conversation

So you made it this far. The person has accepted your invite. You've done all of the research. And finally you are ready to actually *have* the conversation. This is the part of the entire process that will separate success from failure. Where all of the preparation comes together. Many people get nervous at the thought of actually meeting some of the people they have outlined as being critical to the strategy. Well, aside from all of the pointers in Chapter 5 about how to manage yourself, it is important to take comfort in the fact that most experts say nervousness comes primarily from a feeling of lack of preparation. Everyone may experience some level of nervous energy regardless, but in most cases the more prepared you are, the less nervous you will ultimately feel when everything begins. With understanding how to masterfully conduct a coffee conversation, you will feel like a certified professional. The person you are meeting with will feel the same way.

The coffee conversation, when done correctly, is actually a very intricate and sophisticated affair. Almost like a play or a symphony where you are the maestro orchestrating the entire event. Every part of the conversation has been planned down to the smallest detail, even the improvisation is pre-meditated. Sound strange? It's not. Remember, you are having these conversations to accomplish things that are very important to your life's goals and you don't want to leave anything to chance. The

The Coffee Conversation, when done correctly, is actually a very intricate and sophisticated event where even the smallest details are planned

greater your preparation, the greater your likelihood of success.

To understand the format of the Coffee Conversation, and really any business conversation regardless of location, there are three main phases:

1. Opening the Gate
2. Creating Connections
3. Delivering the Pitch.

It is important to note there are no specific time lengths for each phase. As with any conversation, the entire situation must remain completely fluid. Meaning, you will need to gauge and respond based on the other person you are conversing with. They will give you the queues – knowingly or unknowingly - to let you know when they are ready to move to the next phase. As you move with grace between each phase, they will notice and appreciate your mastery, focus, and overall ability to navigate. You

"Precision of communication is important, more important than ever, in our era of hair trigger balances, when a false or misunderstood word may create as much disaster as a sudden thoughtless act."

— James Thurber

will appear confident, intelligent, and fully capable. All qualities that naturally attract others (more on that later). Your attention to their energy will also not be overlooked. The psychological principle of reciprocity applies whether a person does it knowingly or not. It's a natural reaction.

Now we will begin to walk through each phase of the Coffee Conversation. Take your time to understand each step, it is similar to understanding the process of writing a script for a movie or a book. For each conversation you have, especially when there is a definitive purpose or objective, make sure your time counts and your guest enjoys the time with you. Remember, always be giving, and always be adding value.

Opening the Gate

Opening the Gate is the first phase of the Coffee Conversation and is exactly as it sounds. It is the opening of the conversation between two people that have rarely, or in some cases never met. It is very brief, it creates the first impression which takes only seconds to form. This phase of the conversation usually lasts no more than 1 to 3 minutes. With that, you understand there is only a small window, and only one, to get it right. Opening the Gate successfully is so critical, it absolutely CANNOT be understated. It can determine the outcome of everything. It's almost as if the game-winning shot can be taken at the very beginning of the game instead of in the final seconds.

A series of experiments by Princeton psychologists Janine Willis and Alexander Todorov reveal that all it takes is a tenth of a second to form an impression of a stranger from their face, and that longer exposures don't significantly alter those impressions (although they might boost your confidence in your judgments). Their research is presented in their article "First Impressions," in the July issue of Psychological Science.

Whenever two people meet for the first time there is that awkward first few exchanges where the two people are trying to gauge each other and find some sense of common ground. It has been well-documented throughout the field of behavioral science regarding all of the decisions and pre-judgements that take place in this opening sequence. In fact, entire deals may be decided within the first 5 minutes before even getting to the actual presentations! This is why knowing how to successfully open the gate in any coffee conversation is so critical. If done right, it can set the stage for a healthy, vibrant, successful dialogue. If missed, you can spend the remainder of the conversation trying to regain your footing and never quite get there. When it's all over, this will be one of the main points in the entire discussion *you both* remember.

Opening the Gate is an art, and there are three key points you need to follow to make sure you do it successfully.

1. **Eye Contact & Energy**

   At the initial handshake or hello, you need to send the right message. Throughout this entire sequence, you have to take control of your nonverbal communication to make sure you are sending the right message. Eye Contact & Energy has two principles:

- Don't Look Away

- Step-in to Your Handshake or Hello.

You'll notice that some politicians even add to this by doing what is called the 'Deep-Elbow Move'. This is where you shake the hand and reach-in with the other to slightly touch the other persons' elbow. It communicates confidence, openness, compassion, honesty, and many other important traits necessary to create trust.

2. Smile & Radiate

The goal of this principle is obvious but not often followed. You will be surprised how, in the moment, especially if we are a bit nervous, so many people forget the most powerful tool human beings have to communicate safety, honesty, and trust - Smile.

There are a couple of points to note however. The type of smile you use will depend very heavily on the environment you are in. If you are meeting an investor, you won't want to give the same type of wide-eyed smile you would give to a friend you hadn't seen in years. If you did, it would seem forced, slightly inappropriate, and somewhat fake – which would have the opposite effect.

If you are meeting what could be considered 'senior executive' types, a slightly delayed smile the moment after the handshake is a solid way of communicating strength and confidence, while also sending warmth.

3. Be Positive Forever

This is absolutely NOT a no-brainer. I cannot count how many times I have met someone for the first time and at the onset of the conversation, they begin to complain about the food, the weather, their personal selves, or some other issue. Many people make the mistake of feeling like the easiest way to bond is by throwing out something to complain about. This is a *huge* mistake, and sends the absolute wrong signal especially right at the onset of the dialogue (or at any stage). Even if the other person joins-in, most people don't like complainers and victims. Always be positive and find positive

"There is no personal charm so great as the charm of a cheerful temperament."

— Henry Van Dyke

things to say or refer to in your first meeting.

4. Prepare Your Opening – Word-for-Word

This is the part where nothing is left to chance. At first it might sound strange but if you think you can just plop down in the chair and let the bullets fly, you are sorely mistaken. Even the most seasoned communicators prepare opening content for meetings, interviews, and presentations. Don't think for a second that talk show hosts and professional interviewers just sit down and 'wing-it'. They absolutely do not. Most people would be amazed at the amount of preparation that goes into each interview. And how that preparation allows for the entire exchange to appear so enjoyable, natural, and full of good energy.

Keep in mind the opening phase is entirely separate from the actual content you plan to discuss.

It isn't a stretch to write this down and rehearse it line-for-line. Use your research and have an opening ready to make sure you kick-off the conversation with the right tone and energy. In all likelihood, the lines won't come out exactly as you rehearsed them, but it will provide the insurance policy you need.

5. Get Them to Say "Yes" – About Anything

This is also a method many people may have heard of, but very few ever use. Once you get a person in the mindset of saying 'yes', that mindset carries over into everything else in your conversation. It's positive energy, and once you begin to build momentum around that, it can be very difficult for a person to shift gears, even if they want to. Use your research and structure some dialogue that will lead them into agreeing with you and actually saying the word 'yes'. As simple as this seems, it is very powerful.

Remember, Opening the Gate is all about setting a positive tone, creating the right mood, and generating a sense of trust on the part of the person(s) you are conversing with.

In this brief 1 to 3 minutes you can create what is called the *Decision Point of Origin*. This means you will either be working from a 'Yes' decision point, where the person feels a sense of confidence and receptiveness to you and your ideas. Or a decision point of 'No',

Decision Point of Origin: The opening mind-set of the person you are talking to. It can be negative ("No") or positive ("Yes") depending on how you open the conversation

where they get a feeling of a lack of confidence, openness, and trust.

If you don't remember anything else, remember these three words – Nail the Introduction. Shamelessly rehearse. Successfully *Opening the Gate* is the key to accomplishing your objectives in any coffee conversation.

Create Connections

Once you have successfully navigated the opening sequence you have gotten past the toughest part, and now you have only two more phases. In fact, with a solid opening you might find the person you are conversing with will walk through the next phase entirely by themselves.

Creating Connections is the bridge to your main objective and is all about building rapport. If you have ever seen two strangers meet, only to find they are from the same city, possibly went to the same school, and maybe even had some of the same teachers – the overall energy of the conversation takes on an entirely different tone and level of comfort. They begin to communicate as if they have known each other for years. Possibly even ending with a 'Let's stay in touch' gesture. The reason is simple, the more connections you establish with someone the more they are inclined to trust you, support you, and agree with whatever you are trying to accomplish.

How to Create Connections with Anyone

These next six sections outline the most powerful techniques for creating immediate connections with the people you are aiming to meet. Use them in your conversations and you will see how easy it is to establish the rapport you need to build a strong sense of trust, comfort, and credibility when meeting with someone for the first time.

1. Have a Script

After successfully opening the gate, you have no idea where the conversation is going to go. It's fluid, and in all reality you are waiting to see where the other person wants to take it. If they naturally flow into a topic, follow them right in. Remember, the goal is to create the right energy and tone and there is no better way than to let someone speak on a topic they are comfortable with. This will also give you a better gauge of their interests and provide opportunities to connect. Be interested, energetic, and willing to engage them at their point of comfort.

However, sometimes they will not flow into a topic by themselves and might decide to start the conversation with one of the 'canned' questions we are all asked a million times like, "So tell me about yourself." Many of us cringe at being asked this because believe it or not, we have no idea what to say!

I have some good news and some bad news. The bad news is, there is an 80% chance you will be asked this at the beginning of your conversation. Actually – almost *any* conversation. The good news is, you know in advance you are likely to be asked this so, guess what, you can use it as an opportunity to set yourself up to be successful.

Solving this challenge is very simple. Think of the most common questions you are likely to be asked – normally just a handful – and write down your answers word-for-word. Your answers should express exactly what you want to communicate for the situation. After you do this, shamelessly rehearse them just like a Hollywood actor. You want the answer to come out and flow with clarity and confidence. This is also very powerful and will send the right message – you are intelligent, you have clarity, and you know what you are doing. Perfect!

2. Make Them the Focus

Although most people won't admit it, we *all* have a little egotism in our personalities. When you are meeting someone you want to support you in some capacity, always make them the focus. The goal is to establish as many connections with *them* as you possibly can. This will be impossible if you spend the majority of the conversation

You can make more friends in two months by becoming interested in other people than you can in two years by trying to get other people interested in you."

— Dale Carnegie

talking about yourself. This will also ensure the other person is fully engaged, but when you talk about yourself, the other persons' mind is likely to wander. No one's mind wanders when they are entrenched in their own story or a topic they love. Absolutely encourage, and even steer the conversation in such a way that the person is talking about themselves.

3. Become an Active Listener

Being an active listener is critical. The key is not to over, or under do it. When someone is actively listening, they are usually leaning slightly in to engage the other persons' commentary. They give body movements and vocal responses to points being made. You want your energy to slightly match the energy of the other person. I say 'slightly'

"The greatest compliment that was ever paid me was when someone asked me what I thought, and attended to my answer."

— Henry David Thoreau

because you don't want to appear fake when you are meeting someone new. There is always a sensor for authenticity throughout the conversation, especially at the onset, often called the "BS Sensor". Don't overreact to humor or tragedy. Simply be engaged and in-tune. And oh, by the way – checking and answering your cellphone is a conversation killer. The other person won't forget it, especially if they accepted *your* invite. If this meeting is important, put it on silent or leave it in the car. It will kill your entire conversation.

"Listening is a magnetic and strange thing, a creative force. The friends who listen to us are the ones we move toward. When we are listened to, it creates us, makes us unfold and expand."

— Karl Menninger

4. Have Some Back-Up

So maybe they don't go directly into a topic or a standard question. Maybe they just sit there and begin looking around wondering how long they will be stuck with you. Having no idea what to say or where to go next. Ah yes, that ever so brief, supremely awkward moment of silence we have all experienced when you run out of things to talk about with a stranger.

Newsflash, this cannot happen to you! Remember all of that research you did when you were identifying the people you needed to help accomplish your goals? This is the exact part of the process where everything you learned comes into play.

From the research you completed, you will identify interests, past jobs, social endeavors, life experiences, and many other things. When you go into this meeting, you will have at least 4-5 surefire topics prepared to jump into if the other person does not steer the conversation out of the opening gate.

As a part of doing your research on the person to find these points, you will also want to conduct some additional research on the topics themselves. Be able to, at minimum, speak on some surface-level points about the topic. Trust me when I say, if you strike a nerve, 9 times out of 10, the other person will shoot out like a rocket. Firstly, they will be thankful for the lifeline which avoids that universally dreaded awkward moment. Secondly, you will again be on *their* familiar territory, talking about *them* or something *they* enjoy. You will make them comfortable and they will have an overall positive feeling about you and the entire experience of meeting with you.

5. Name-Drop

This is simple but also crucial and probably not what you initially thought. Name-dropping in this context is not blatantly finding any avenue to say a name of someone famous or otherwise important that you might know. Name-dropping here means saying the other persons' name throughout the conversation. Dale Carnegie wrote in his classic book "How to Win Friends and Influence People", "…the one thing people love to hear almost more than anything else is their own name". The key is, you'll want to sprinkle it in. Don't overuse it, or you will risk sounding like a nagging parent. But use it just enough, maybe on key points where it grabs the person, reassures them that you respect them and know who they are. Believe it or not, just saying someone's name even though they know that you already know it, does all of these things.

6. **Know When to Say When**

Said differently, know when enough is enough. Keep in mind through all of this brilliant conversation you haven't actually talked about what you originally intended to invite the person to discuss yet. And this is an important point to be aware of. It was intentional. You never want to rush directly into your 'ask'. There will be no rapport, no trust, and no momentum. You must go through each phase of the Coffee Conversation to win. However, you have to know when to cross the bridge, and enter into your main point.

Remember, the entire process is fluid. There is no set time limit to each phase and you have to pay attention to the signs the other person will knowingly or unknowingly provide to let you know when to call it and move to the next phase of the conversation.

The single most important point to transitioning with the highest probability of success is this - Always transition on a peak. There will be a moment in the Connection phase where the energy is extremely good, the mission has been accomplished, and to go any further would only strain and possibly diminish the bond you've worked so hard to create. When you feel this moment, transition smoothly but effectively into your Pitch. You will have the momentum, you will be starting from a "Yes" Decision Point of Origin, and your likelihood of success could not be any higher.

Always transition on a peak, when the energy of the conversation is at a high point, into the next phase.

Delivering the Pitch

Although the subject of 'How to Pitch an Idea' is not the general topic of this book. It is one of the most critical parts of any Coffee Conversation. If you never ask for what you invited the person to discuss, what would be the point of all of this preparation and strategy. The Pitch is where you get to discuss what you want, so it is important to know how to do it successfully. I would also recommend some additional research and reading on this topic. Because there are so many different business types, scenarios, and objectives - the style, tools, and overall format of your actual pitch will vary widely based upon what you are trying to accomplish. This is something you will want to absolutely master as it is the ultimate determination of success or failure for this entire endeavor.

The Pitch is critical. To deliver a successful pitch, no matter how minor or major it may be, be sure to include these five characteristics in your delivery.

1. **Immediately Strike a Nerve**

    Your opening must be concise, very smooth, and it must immediately appeal to something they can identify with. It could be a noble motive, personal benefit or gain, or indirectly achieving something they would like to be associated with.

    Whatever your 'nerve strike' is, it cannot be subtle or indirect. It must be clear and spelled-out in a very logical and realistic manner.

    The last point being one of the most important. For example, any experienced investor knows that a promise of guaranteed returns of more than 20%, in any business, is probably moonshine. You will lose them quickly. Don't overpromise, but make sure you know exactly which nerve you are going to strike, and you are rehearsed and prepared to do so.

2. Use a Story

The easiest way for most people to understand a concept is when it is placed into a story format. This is how most of us consume information even as adults. Think about it – movies, TV shows, blogs, and magazine articles – all stories.

Connect your pitch into a brief story that will cover the before and after, the benefits, and how it directly applies to something or someone real.

3. Make It Quick

Many people fall down on this point. Your initial foray into your pitch must be very concise. This was mentioned in the last section, but this point is so important it deserves its own section. So many people attempt to dump every single data point into their initial presentation or pitch. You will absolutely fail if you do this. Your entire pitch, from beginning to end must be condensed to no more than 5-7 minutes. Remember, this is a Coffee Conversation and not a full boardroom presentation. Your only objective is to peak their interest, get their approval, and move to the next stage where they ask for more.

Furthermore, after your 5-7 minutes is up, if interested, they will definitely have some questions.

4. Make *Them* the Salesperson

This point connects directly to the previous one. If you deliver a solid pitch and begin to get active questions, you can transition the Q&A into a tone where *they* will begin to give you solutions and options to consider. They might even begin to use the word 'We' in their questions. When you begin to hear this, it's a sure sign things are going well.

5. **Always Be Closing**

Similar to the previous phase 'Create Connections', once you get to the 'Pitch', you want to be in the mind-set of sealing the deal. Don't let the conversation and 'ideation' linger on for too long. Once you feel the energy reaching a high-point, and especially if the other person is actively engaged in the dialogue, move-in for the kill and put forward 'The Ask' you intended for this entire meeting. This is the most sensitive point of the entire conversation, so you will want to be paying attention. You will see it. You will feel it. And when you do, don't hesitate to deliver your close.

This, again, you will want to have prepared and rehearsed.

One Last Piece of Advice

One critical thing to remember is this, never take your mind off of your objective. The goal with this phase is to get the other person to buy-in to your idea or proposal. In all likelihood, every final decision will not be made in this brief sitting. In fact, as mentioned before, if there is interest there will almost certainly be a follow-up meeting to dig-in to the details. This is important to keep in mind.

As you move through the conversation, the other person might arbitrarily throw-out some points you

"The real art of conversation is not only to say the right thing in the right place, but to leave unsaid the wrong thing at the tempting moment."

— Lady Dorothy Nevill

don't agree with, either about your idea or in general. Three words – Let It Go. Whatever you do, do not engage in a confrontational discussion. Certainly not an argument. You will never win, even if you make your point and the other person concedes. You will lose. You are not there to 'be right'. You are in the meeting to achieve a critical part of your overall strategy and life plan. Always ask yourself which is more important.

"Don't fight a battle if you don't gain anything by winning."

— Field Marshal Erwin Rommel

The entire Coffee Strategy is 100% centered around your life's most important goals. The less you leave to chance and good luck, the more likely you are to be successful almost every time. Anyone can win every now and again. It takes time and preparation to win repeatedly - and that my friend, is the goal.

KEY LESSONS

- The Coffee Conversation, when done correctly, is actually a very intricate and sophisticated event where even the smallest details are planned.

- The Coffee Conversation has three parts:

- Opening the Gate

- Creating Connections

- Delivering the Pitch

- The Coffee Conversation is fluid and relies on your ability to pick-up on the others person's signals to know when to move to the next phase.

- Always transition on a high-point in the phase. It can only get worse if you wait.

- Opening the Gate only lasts 1-3 minutes but can determine the success or failure of the entire conversation.

- Create the right 'Decision point of origin' in the conversation.

- Keep the focus on exploring the interests of the other person. Make them the focus.

- The goal is to create as many connections as possible. The more connections you create, the stronger the relationship will become.

- People inherently do not like to say 'No' when they feel good about the relationship and overall conversation.

- The Pitch should be rehearsed to perfection.

- Make your pitch brief and targeted directly on the objective.

- Never engage in an argument or confrontational tone in the conversation - you will never win.

- Close your conversation when the momentum and interest is at the highest point. Keep them wanting more.

Chapter 6

The Most Important Part – You.

Literally everything up to this point has been preparation and planning. Well, I almost hate to say.....that was the easy part. We have now reached the part in the process where the "rubber begins to hit the road". This is the exciting phase where you have to step into your new self, and in many cases, step outside of your comfort zone. But before you jump into making contact and setting your invites, there are some important steps you'll want to take to ensure your success. Again, preparation is the key. There are a number of things that will happen before, during, and after the actual meetings you have. Any misstep can translate into a missed opportunity, or could even spell disaster.

"It's not the will to win that matters—everyone has that. It's the will to prepare to win that matters."
— Paul "Bear" Bryant

To Master Yourself is to Master the World

There has been so much discussion up to this point on identifying your goals and the other people involved. Believe it or not, accomplishing every one of your objectives has just as much, if not more, to do with _you_ than anything else.

What if everything went exactly as you planned? Are you ready to have those meetings? Are you prepared to step on this newly created stage where the stakes are as high as they have ever been?

This is where many people get 'cold-feet' and begin to procrastinate. So lets' walk through the most important things you will need to work on _within yourself_ to make sure that when you are placed in position, you come out on top.

"Sometimes we have the dream but we are not ourselves ready for the dream. We have to grow to meet it."
— Louis L'Amour

Presence - The Secret to Attracting Anything.

"It may be difficult to define, but we all know presence when we encounter it. Someone walks into the room and people step aside. Heads turn. When those with presence speak, people listen. When they ask, people answer. When they lead, people follow."
— *Dianna Booher*

Presence is for many, one of those elusive concepts not often understood. At the same time, it is the very thing that has so many of us wondering why certain people just seem to 'naturally' attract things to themselves. Whether it is people, jobs, opportunities, or even random conversation at the grocery store, these individuals seem to be magnets attracting positive energy and as a result, things just seem to fall into their laps.

The good news is, it isn't as 'random' as you think. In fact, most of us have the ability to do the same thing. It's called having 'presence'.

An entire book can be written on the topic of presence alone. It is a very powerful skill, and is worth the time and investment to pursue a deep understanding of. After completing this book, I would recommend that you go online or purchase some additional books to continue your mastery of this skill. This chapter will give you what you need to know to master the coffee conversation and how to have presence right away.

There are three forms of presence – internal, external, and verbal. Each one is very powerful. In fact, mastering just one of these will have a huge impact on your life, so imagine mastering all three.

Inner presence: The way that you experience yourself – internally.

Internal Presence

Before we get into discussing internal presence, it is important for you to know the definition. Internal presence can be described as the way that you experience yourself – internally. The way to think, make decisions, work with others, your self-thoughts (doubts), your inner talk and how it makes you feel from moment to moment. That is your inner presence. And although it appears to be completely internal, it translates into many things that happen on the outside in almost every area of your life. Internal presence is one of the most important things you can have. When considering the areas of your life it can impact, you begin to understand why. When you have internal presence you immediately become more credible, your points are taken as truths in meetings, you are centered and there is a natural confidence about you. This is one of the most attractive qualities any person can have. People are drawn to it. Your physical appearance actually becomes secondary in the moment and you will find it much easier to get your way with large groups of people.

The most common challenge with Internal Presence is controlling nervous energy.

"Nothing is a greater impediment to being on good terms with others than being ill at ease with yourself."
— Honoré de Balzac

How Do You Develop Internal Presence?

Some people have a bit of a head start as they may have learned this behavior at some point in their lives and are a little further along than most. The good news is, very few people deliberately practice this craft and generally believe either you 'have it' or you don't. This misunderstanding creates a huge opportunity for you as you begin to develop this skill.

The three most important steps to developing Internal Presence:

1. **Learning to Stay Calm**

   This is in almost all situations. Think about politicians (and temporarily disregard your feelings about them for sake of the point). The one thing you will notice whenever they are speaking is, they always attempt to smile whenever possible. And in the most

"The first and best victory is to conquer self."
— Plato

extreme circumstances, they are always calm, composed, and completely under control.

On the other side, have you ever been in a meeting where two people were debating opposing views, and even though one person may have had the stronger point – they lost control of their emotions, and as a result, their point was also disregarded. These are two opposite extremes just to give you the full perspective of the point. The most common challenge to maintaining presence for 99% of people is just plain getting nervous. You might be making a solid point in a meeting, giving a presentation, or getting to the point of asking for the sale, and your nerves begin to fire-up and in some cases they can even take over. We have all been through or have seen what happens next –

stuttering commentary, mental black-out, heart-pounding, voice-cracking, fidgeting, sweating, and a whole host of other things. It's a nightmare. This will absolutely kill your momentum. Nervous energy is like reverb on a microphone, people naturally avoid it and whoever projects it.

However, once you learn to stay calm in all situations, you will be shocked and amazed at how powerful and rare this skill is. Even if you do nothing else in this entire book, mastering this skill will change your life.

2. **Diet:**

Strangely enough, one of the most common causes of situational anxiety and stage-fright is diet. There are a number of things you eat and drink on a regular basis that increase your cortisol levels. Cortisol is the stress hormone that kicks in when you are in danger. It's almost pure adrenaline. It causes your heart rate to increase, shuts down or severely limits certain functions of your brain (which is why you blackout) and essentially puts you in the mode of trying to escape from danger. It doesn't matter that you are just speaking in front of a harmless group of people. Does this sound familiar?

Things to avoid or reduce in your diet if you suffer from severe anxiety when speaking, or just prior to any situation where you tend to get nervous:

a. Caffeine
b. Sugar
c. Trans Fats
d. Vegetable & Seed Oils
e. Fruit Juices

f. Alcohol

Things to add to your diet to reduce cortisol and the likelihood of anxiety

a. Aswaghanda

b. Rhodiolla

c. Kava Kava

d. Vitamin C

e. Zinc

f. Spinach

g. Citrus Fruits

h. Mini-Greens

i. Holy Basil

j. Many more

3. **Exercise & Sleep**

This one might be more obvious but you would be surprised by the number of people that ignore its value. Exercise reduces stress and can remove stress hormones from your body. This is especially important if you have a major event coming up.

Getting a good night's sleep prior to any major event is extremely critical. The common behavior is surprisingly the exact opposite, staying up all night cramming and reviewing points. Don't do this. Be sure to do your preparation leading up to the moment. The night before, get a good night's sleep.

4. Meditation

Some people think meditation is just for monks but it isn't. Meditation is one of the best ways to achieve personal balance. Some of the best athletes and business leaders from around the world have all used meditation to help them overcome fears, visualize success, and gain their inner sense of calm in all situations. It can literally be as simple as finding a quiet space, focusing on your breathing, and just letting your mind relax. I personally recommend taking a step further by visualizing the entire situation you are preparing for, even a simple meeting, and seeing yourself being successful. The positive impact is unbelievable.

5. **Develop Your Self-Esteem**

More than confidence. Self-esteem is the internal belief that you belong. Most anxiety or discomfort comes from an internal feeling that you don't belong in the environment you find yourself in and you are somehow 'unworthy' of the situation. You must always realize that whatever situation you are in, you deserve to be there. Make sure you conduct some additional research on how to continuously develop your personal self-esteem. You would be surprised

"No man can make you feel inferior without your consent."
— *Eleanor Roosevelt*

that some of the people you 'think' either do not, or have never had this challenge actually work on this every day.

6. **Personal Mantra**

   Pick three words you will use to define yourself. Limit to only three. Write them down and read them to yourself on a regular, even daily, basis. Live them vehemently. These words define you – to others and to yourself. Make everything you do always reflect those words.

   "Public opinion is a weak tyrant compared with our own private opinion. What a man thinks of himself, that is which determines, or rather indicates, his fate."
   — Henry David Thoreau

7. **Practice**

   This is a no-brainer but must consciously be done. Find situations where you can practice your internal presence. This is where stepping out of your comfort zone will be required. Join Toastmasters, or an interest group, volunteer to deliver presentations at work, make an active effort to always participate in meetings. This practice will prepare you and allow you to master controlling your internal energy. When the true moment actually comes, you will find that your 'presence' will also come naturally.

"While others were out partying, I was training. While they were out dancing at the clubs, I was training... and training... and training."
— Arnold Schwarzenegger

Important Note:
On this journey in developing your personal presence. You will begin to notice how liberating and powerful this skill actually is. Be sure not to go too far in your social 'fearlessness' where natural confidence becomes perceived as arrogance and conceit. It will backfire. Remember to stay balanced.

External Presence

External presence is not as one dimensional as internal presence because it actually has two primary parts that must be considered to be complete.

The first part of external presence is the most obvious, how you look. The way you dress, groom, your body language, and overall posture all combine together to describe how you 'appear' to others.

Most people overlook or completely miss the second part of external presence – how you make others feel.

Both aspects of external presence, although completely separate, are equally as important and impactful on how you are perceived by others.

Developing Your External Presence

A good place to start when thinking about how to develop your external presence is

External Presence: External presence describes how the world experiences, or perceives you. The overall impression that others might form of you after a dialogue or witnessing an exchange is the outcome of your presence.

asking yourself a series of questions and writing down the answers. I must say, the key to this exercise is being completely honest with yourself even if you don't like the answers you know to be true. If you struggle, ask someone close to you who will be honest to help.

Question #1
What do I want people to perceive when they see me and interact with me?

This goes back to beginning with the end in mind. And this will be different for different people and depends entirely on your objective. The point is, you will be making a conscious choice and taking control of your image. Something not many people are cognizant of doing. Think about the bigger goals you've already outlined. Now think about how your current image is either in, or out of sync with accomplishing that goal. It is important to note that we are not talking about dressing up in a costume to achieve your goals. As we will note later, authenticity is a key part of external presence as well. But obviously, if your goal is completely out of sync with your image, some changes will have to be made. And quite possibly, these changes will transition your image to closer reflect who you truly are or aspire to become. And that is the most authentic image you could have.

Question #2
What do people currently perceive when they look at my external presence?

Another way to phrase this question is, "how would someone describe me?" Think about your co-workers, friends, business partners, the cashier at the grocery store you frequent. This is the question that requires the highest degree of self-reflection and honesty on your part. You may need to take some time to reflect in order to answer this one properly – and it is extremely important to get it right.

Knowing how people would describe you will allow you to know how far you have to go, and in which areas, to adjust your external presence to align with your goals. You might be unaware of how people perceive you – possibly because someone said "it doesn't matter what people think" at some point in your life to instill confidence. You may have developed a tone-deaf attitude towards how other experience you. First, let's address the misconception around the concept of "it doesn't matter what people think". It is a valid thought and overall approach, but it also has a certain application. You would want to invoke that principle when you are forging through starting a new business or idea, or if you are surrounded by people who doubt you or mock you for trying or being different. In those cases, you must discard what those foolish people are saying, and forge ahead based solely on what you know and believe

"Keep away from people who belittle your ambitions. Small people always do that, but the really great make you feel that you, too, can become great."
— Mark Twain

to be true. However, in the general everyday application of interacting with people who do not have ill-intent towards you - people who you will be working or interacting with, people who might support or otherwise invest in your ideas, yes - it actually DOES matter what they think of you. And you want to control that perception as best you can so as to secure the desired outcome.

Question #3
Do you have too much, or too little external presence?

This question might require a little explanation to answer it properly. There are three types of people in almost every room. There is the person that:

- Talks Too Much: Has something to say about everything. Tries to dominate every conversation. Can be a bit over the top. Needs the spot light.

- Talks Too Little: The invisible person. Literally disappears in the room. The spectator that rarely shares an opinion that others value or notice.
- The Balanced Person: When they talk people listen. They know when to talk and when to listen.

The obvious choice is you want to be the balanced person. But you need to be honest with yourself and identify which person you are *currently*.

Question#4
Do people like dealing with you? And do they perceive you as being credible when they do?

These two questions do not require a great deal of explanation, but are critical to your overall ability to persuade and communicate effectively with others.

Likeability: Do people like dealing with you?

Credibility: Do people respect you, and respect your statements, opinions, and overall judgement?

Complete these three exercises by giving deep and honest thought to answering each one of the questions. Take your time and write down your answers. Once you do this, analyze the gaps between where you currently are, and where you are trying to go. As you read through the rest of this chapter, use the concepts to map out a plan for how you will transition your external presence into the type you are striving to project.

The Three Dimensions of External Presence

External presence has three primary dimensions you will need to focus on for mastery – facial warmth, vocal warmth and body warmth. All three combine to create your complete external presence.

You will notice the concepts all center around 'warmth'. This is absolutely intentional so you will understand the overall objective of the concept. This is not just about appearances, equally important in your external presence is the energy you radiate. The most powerful type in communications being – warmth. This is the type of feeling you get when you meet a stranger and they immediately make you feel comfortable. They somehow help others navigate their nervous energy to arrive at a mutual safe place where everyone feels respected and comfortable – said differently, they project warmth and make others feel that way as well.

Always keep in mind the concept of likeability is often perceived the wrong way. In most cases, it is not that people don't like you. The real issue is that, for some reason, they don't think you like them. When you project warmth, it immediately dispels this notion and causes people to respond in kind. Even if they really don't like you! It's powerful.

Facial Warmth

Facial warmth is actually one of the easiest things to fix. It's also one of the largest tell-tale signs of your overall state of being. It comes down to one very simple concept — smile.

If you are often asked by coworkers "what's wrong?" or "wow, what are you concentrating on…?" Then you know that your general facial expression might be one that is a bit stern and serious. Think about projecting a more balanced expression on your face, especially when meeting or interacting with others. A stern face is essentially the same as a brick wall. It tells others not to approach, or at least that is how it is normally perceived.

At the same time, you don't want to have a fake smile plastered on your face at every venue. You are not a gameshow host. Don't go over the top as if someone just told a joke. Be balanced. There is a time when a thoughtful or even a serious look is completely appropriate and even necessary. The point here is to be aware of your natural face, and when meeting and interacting with others, a smile is the best way to project warmth.

Facial Warmth Exercise:

This is a powerful exercise I have used and many actors, business people, politicians, and others have practiced with their facial warmth.

1. Look at yourself in a mirror.
2. Place your index fingers at the corners of your mouth.
3. Shift the corners of your mouth slightly upwards. Hold them there, then remove them.
4. Say hello to your new 'natural' facial expression.

What you have done with this ever so slight move is activate two of the 80 muscles in your cranium – your *levator labiis*. These muscles connect your mouth to your eyes. When you perform this small move, you give yourself just the hint of a smile. Faint, but visible. It makes you look warm, confident, upbeat, and inviting. Exactly what you are trying to accomplish with your facial warmth.

Vocal Warmth

Vocal warmth is something that can be developed for a lifetime. There are entire industries around helping people develop their voices. Some people have even stated, the oratory skill (public speaking), is the single most powerful skill on the planet earth – and I would agree. But we all have to start somewhere in our journey.

The first thing to realize is that our voices sound different to others than they do to us. Think back to the first (or last) time you heard yourself on a recording. What was

"We often refuse to accept an idea merely because the tone of voice in which it has been expressed is unsympathetic to us."
— Friedrich Nietzsche

your first response? "That doesn't sound like me!?" When thinking about your vocal warmth and overall external presence, there are some easy-to-follow points to keep in mind whenever you are speaking.

- **Situational Awareness**: Make sure your tone of voice matches the environment you are in. Have you ever been somewhere where there was a person conversing with someone (either in person or over the phone) and everyone within a 50ft radius could hear them? If asked, they might just reply with something like "I'm just a loud person." Well, in this category 'loud' can come off as obnoxious, rude, insensitive, etc. If they are speaking directly to you, they can appear to be self-centered and conceited. Obviously you do not want to project any of these.

The converse is also true. Someone in a meeting might speak so low that barely anyone can hear them. Situational awareness means you take into consideration the environment you are speaking in and adjust the volume of your voice to match the situation.

Voice Inflection: This is a common factor that most people understand. Using voice inflection means you vary the pitch of your voice based on the point you are making. You want to punch your points through, maybe not to the extent of a news anchor, as that doesn't go over so well in person. But you never want your voice to taper off at the end of your sentences. Breathe-in to your sentences and words to give them life.

"They may forget what you said, but they will never forget how you made them feel."
— Carl W. Buechner

You also want to avoid speaking in flat tones that have no change – a monotone voice. You will put everyone to sleep.

- **Pace**: For most of us who have not reflected on our speaking styles, we have only one pace when speaking. For some people it's fast – and they are known as fast talkers. For others it is slow – and they are known as slow talkers. You may have a habitual tendency to be one or the other just from years of personality development. But now that you are transitioning into a space of awareness, varying the pace of your speaking to match the content you are communicating is a very effective method for keeping your audiences' (one person or many) attention throughout your dialogue.

Body Warmth

Body warmth is probably the most externally-focused area of your external presence. To demonstrate body warmth, you will want to be aware of three primary areas – your posture, your actual appearance, and your overall body language. For most people these are the easiest areas of external presence to identify and correct. Your posture and overall body language go hand in hand. One compliments and is indelibly intertwined with the other. However, they can still be assessed and reviewed separately to make sure they are correctly understood.

Your posture can be understood as how you position your body. Do you sit upright? Or do you hunch over or slouch? If you want to win at projecting the best external

"Body language is a very powerful tool. We had body language before we had speech, and apparently, 80% of what you understand in a conversation is read through the body, not the words."
— Deborah

presence there are some very easy things you can start doing immediately.

- **Don't Slouch**. This means 'hunching-over' or having an inward curve from your shoulders to your waist. This posture gives off a sense of low self-esteem or lack of confidence. Always sit or stand erect, not like a superhero, but in a natural upright posture. This tells people you are confident.

- **No Fidgeting**. This often plagues people when delivering public presentations. Keep your hands and feet still. Avoid scratching your face or head, shifting your body frequently, or otherwise having an excessive amount of movement with your body that does not compliment the point you are making. It's distracting.

Your overall appearance is just that, how you dress and look. If you are about to meet one of the important people on your list, you don't want to wear a tuxedo, but you also don't want to look like you just threw something on. Even more so if this is a formal presentation. There is a fundamental concept of reciprocity in human nature – when people feel like you have taken the time to respect their time, in most cases, they will do the same.

Dress the part, look the part, and feel the part. Don't leave anything to chance. The more you are aware of your external presence, the more natural you will become. Thus, you will begin to attract and impact others in the ways that you are striving to achieve.

KEY LESSONS

- Accomplishing every one of your objectives has just as much if not more to do with you than anything else.

- Having 'Presence' is one of the secrets to attracting anything you pursue in life.

- Presence is NOT natural, but it can be developed over time like any other skill.

- There are two types of presence - Internal Presence & External Presence.

- Internal presence is defined as how you experience or feel about yourself in different situations.

- Diet and exercise can have a significant impact on your internal presence.

- External presence is defined as not only how you look but also how you make others feel.

- External presence has 3 parts - facial warmth, vocal warmth, and body warmth.

Chapter 7

How to Build Your Brand

In addition to all of the powerful and interesting methods and strategies you have been learning over the past few chapters, there is another dimension of your 'You' that you must take into consideration. We live in a time where everyone has their own individual platform for communicating to the world. If used and managed successfully, it can be a hidden force that helps you in everything you do. If not, it can undermine your goals and objectives as it will communicate a message that is contradictory to the one message you are looking to deliver.

Your personal brand is your public image, and whether we like it or not, everyone has one. In fact, we are almost at a point in this social era where, if you *do not* have one, there may be suspicions that you have something to hide! Wow!

That is both good and bad. The bad thing is, some of us are by nature, very private individuals. Maybe we describe ourselves as introverts. Or maybe we have not yet decided to 'jump-in' to the social media arena with all of our personal business.

The good news is, once you make the decision to step out-there, even just a little, it can go a very long way in controlling, managing, and reinforcing your personal brand to the world. In some ways it might be better that you haven't stepped out yet because, maybe you have avoided making the mistakes others have made as a result of not understanding the power and permanence of the social media landscape. This gives you the ability to enter into this space the right way and take control from the very beginning.

In either case, my advice is to use this new paradigm to your advantage. In all likelihood, anyone you meet for the first time will be very inclined to do a web search on your name. Possibly right from their phone in the car before or after you meet to see what comes up. How powerful would it be if everything they find reinforces the exact image you reflect in your meeting? That's how it's done. Some call it the Bee-Sting Effect, a very persuasive marketing strategy that can be used for just about anything, including yourself.

As with some of the other critical concepts and strategies in this book, I recommend taking your personal brand very seriously. As such, ongoing and continued research for tools, methods, and other ways to continuously improve in this area

Bee Sting Effect: A phenomenon where a marketer will look to use multiple channels collectively to reinforce a single message. The thought being, the more a person sees the message, in different ways, the more they will believe and react in the way the message is communicating.

throughout your personal journey is highly recommended. But you also need to get started right away.

9 Ways to Build a Powerful Personal Brand

It is important to understand while walking through this entire development cycle, not one of these points is a 'one-and-done'. Meaning, these are meant to be patterns of behavior that are consistently done to continue nurturing and building your brand.

In the current economic environment we live in, whether you are in business for yourself, or if you have a career, you are in fact a free-agent. Whether you know it or not, you have a personal brand. Very similar to your external presence, people will perceive you in a branded way that you can either control, or allow to happen. Here are some of the most powerful personal attributes you can use to turn this reality into a huge strategic asset that will propel you forward, even while you sleep.

1. **Listen First, Then Be Heard**

    People will love you for this as so many people struggle, internally or externally, to be heard and understood. Make this a habit and a hallmark of who you are. Listening first, then being heard means to empathize with the other person. Let them tell their story. Make them the focal point. And as we mentioned before, build more connections with them. This will solidify any relationship and make you a person others feel comfortable around. To clarify, this doesn't mean you become a martyr where your voice is never heard. It just means you don't immediately make yourself the only thing you are interested in. Allow others to shine, encourage it, and then get to your points or topics.

2. Be Interesting

Many people don't think about this. Maybe because it sounds so simple. Being interesting is having something to talk about. Have a hobby that you can explain to someone. Have an interest, be it reading, bike riding, or anything else. Everyone loves to learn and hear an experience told through someone else's personal lense. Movies make billions of dollars every year using this very idea.

"That which you or I think is most unique about ourselves we hide. In ordinary discourse, in the normal state, we share our common self, our superficial self. Yet what is most unique about us is what has the greatest potential for bonding us. When we share our uniqueness, we discover the commonality in greatness that defines everyone on the planet."

— Robert E. Quinn

Being interesting doesn't mean you have to be the center of the party. The person with the entire crowd huddled around them while telling some super unrealistic tale of mastery.

It means being up on current events, being diverse, having an opinion and not being afraid to share it. And then having something personal about yourself that allows other to get an added view into who you are.

The easiest way to do this is to have a few stories up your sleeve that you can tell at any given time. They can be rehearsed. Doesn't matter if you've told them one hundred times. Sometimes the person will ask you to tell it again just because they like it (like watching an old movie). Be interesting.

3. Be a Resource

As you begin to execute on your Coffee Strategy, you will begin to meet a wide variety of people. These are people that many others may not have the courage, or take the time to meet with. This puts you in a very powerful position of knowing many different people, knowing their hobbies and interests, their goals and other even personal details.

As you meet people, you will hear needs and aspirations surface. Don't hesitate to make connections with other people you have met that might help them move their goals further along. This is how you add value into the relationship. This is also how you ensure your phone calls are always answered or returned. You will begin to get invited places unexpectedly, or others will do the same for you and you will begin to receive help from places you didn't expect. Be a Resource.

4. Specialize and Become Invaluable

Many of us have a wide variety of interests. Ever hear a kid explain how they want to be an astronaut, a professional soccer player, a rock star, and a fireman when they grow up? Well, to be completely honest, some of us, even as adults, are very similar. The key to honing in and having immense value to others is to specialize in a few core areas. This doesn't mean you have to give up everything else. It means that you have taken an inventory of all of your interests and capabilities, and you have selected the ones you are best at, have the highest probability of success and influence in, and you spend the majority of your time becoming an expert in that particular space.

"If you chase two rabbits, both will escape"

— Unknown

143

This point is actually one of the most important out of this entire list. Don't be scattered. If you become known for being an expert in a specific area, you will become sought after in your field of interest and the goals you have written down will in many cases 'come to you' as opposed to your pursuing them.

5. **Polish Your Social Profiles**

We discussed this in one of the previous sections, but the point cannot be overemphasized. You will be surprised what some of our social media profiles look like and the image they convey. Either abandoned, or maybe still look like it would if we were in high school or college. Undertake an effort to complete a massive overhaul of your social presence. Doesn't mean change who you are or disconnect all of your friends. Just make sure whatever is out there aligns with your goals and objectives and what you are looking to project. This is very important because in many cases, a person can decide to take your meeting or not take it, based solely on what they see online.

6. Connect Often

Connections are just that, connections. And like any form of connection, they can grow stronger or weaker based on whether or not they are maintained. Whenever you establish a solid association with someone, you don't always have to have a coffee meetup or lunch with them, you might simply forward them a link to an article you read that you know interests them. Maybe the score to a game with a silly note. Or maybe just a 'hey how are you' text message. The easiest is a note on special days. Whatever it is, make it a regular part of your routine. Make notes and set reminders on your phone or calendar. They key here is to never let connections run dry. You never know when you might need to call someone, and the worst thing is to be perceived as only calling when you need something. You are likely to feel a little resentment from the other person. Even if you don't feel it, know for sure it's there. Connect Often.

7. Give Credit Publicly

Don't be fooled. Everyone - that is....EVERYONE loves to receive credit for things they have done, ideas they have offered, or things they have been a part of. And they love it even more when they receive that credit in public. They might assume the modest "you didn't have to" posture, but always understand this is one of the most powerful things you can do. Especially in front of loved ones or others they are looking to make an impression upon. You can even give credit to others on your social profiles. Some platforms like LinkedIn allow you to give recommendations. Take advantage of this. The only point of note is you want your recommendation and endorsement to have value. Make people work for it. Saying thank you and giving credit is one thing, offering up a full endorsement is another. If you give everyone the same treatment, no one will feel unique, and thus your endorsement will lose value. Nevertheless – give credit, and do it publicly.

8. **Don't Keep Score**

This is a fatal flaw and you would be surprised how many people do it. I am told this is actually a part of the culture in some cities like Hollywood. Maybe it works there, but everywhere else on the planet, this is a huge no-no. Keeping score means you keep mental notes on everything you have done for others. Maybe not all bad, but don't mention it in conversation or in asking for a return favor. Never do this, unless it is your intent to sever or weaken the relationship afterwards. Because that is exactly what it will do. The other person will resent you for it, and in some cases, not want to accept (or give) any additional favors from you.

9. Don't have a Disposable Network

Not having a disposable network further emphasizes the point of connecting often but in a different way. Throughout your journey you will come across people who will help you in both minor and major ways. Others will just be acquaintances you meet that may or may not offer anything of extreme value. The point here is, never receive a favor from someone and neglect to come back to say thank you. This will certainly kill any future favors or connections you might want to make with that individual in the future. Also, when you express gratitude, don't completely dispose of that person. Follow-up. Let them know how things went. Whether things went good or not so good. You will be surprised to learn they might have some additional 'help' up their sleeves to offer you. Or maybe 5 years from now you might need them again. It's a small world, and the price of an occasional 'Hello' is a small price to pay for maintaining the value of a strong personal network.

KEY LESSONS

- Understand that whether we like it or not, we are all an individual brand.

- Building your individual brand can help you accomplish your goals even while you sleep.

- Almost everyone you meet is likely to search your name online to see what comes up. Use this to your advantage.

- Seven things you can do to build a powerful brand

  - Listen First, then be Heard

  - Be Interesting

  - Be a Resource

  - Polish Your Social Profiles

  - Connect Often

  - Give Credit Publicly

  - Don't Keep Score

  - Don't Have a Disposable Network

Chapter 8

Bringing It All Together

So here we are at the end, which, in reality is just the beginning. We have entered into a new era of human interaction which has also brought with it a new definition of what is means to "be social".

The coffeehouse is now a permanent fixture of our, now more than ever, social society. What began only a few years ago as a trend has now become a cultural norm. Going to the coffeehouse, sitting down either alone, with friends, or with business associates – is now as normal as going to a drive-thru to get a burger.

The benefit of any new cultural phenomenon which has occurred at this scale is, it also creates new opportunities for everyone.

"What's Your Coffee Strategy?" was written to help you define, understand, and taking advantage of the opportunities the modern coffee culture has created.

The one thing that has always been true about goals is they are all completely achievable and they all look good on paper. What many of us did not understand (before reading this book) is how to take those goals from the pages we wrote them on and - using the coffeehouse - implement a comprehensive strategy to achieve them.

As we discussed in earlier chapters, writing the goals is not even the first step. The first step is truly looking into ourselves and understanding the underlying premises of our goals to understand what goals to commit ourselves to. This is one of the most common mistakes. After reading this book, I know we now understand how to avoid it.

Another wall so many of us fall short of climbing after we document the goals is, understanding how to navigate the social interactions required to achieve them. Who do we need? How do we get a meeting? When the meeting occurs, what do we say? How can we ask strangers for help and expect to be successful? These questions are where many of us stumble. Most of us can figure out what we want in life. It's navigating the ultra-complex web of social engagements, meetings, conversations, and sales pitches that we may not know how to work through or may be downright terrified of. The latter half of this book was dedicated to walking you through each step of this complex maze, even down to how to structure the 'Coffee Conversation'. If you follow this game plan, you will be amazed at how easily you can be successful at this stage of your journey.

Finally, goal achievement is not necessarily the only thing the concepts in this book are written for. You can use these principles in so many ways to improve your everyday social interactions with others. Remember, the coffeehouse is the new hub for social exchanges. Not all are centered around business or life goals, you may just want to meet new people, or catch up with a friend. For many of us, these social interactions with new people – or people we haven't seen in a while – can take us outside of our comfort zones. Use the strategies of engagement and conversation outlined in this book to improve your confidence. You will be amazed at how much the overall quality of your social interactions improves. Life is not just about accomplishing goals, objectives, and life missions.......you also want to have fun along the way.

Go forth and conquer.

www.ingramcontent.com/pod-product-compliance
Lightning Source LLC
Chambersburg PA
CBHW021931190326
41519CB00009B/981